THE BEST NBA GUARDS OF ALL TIME

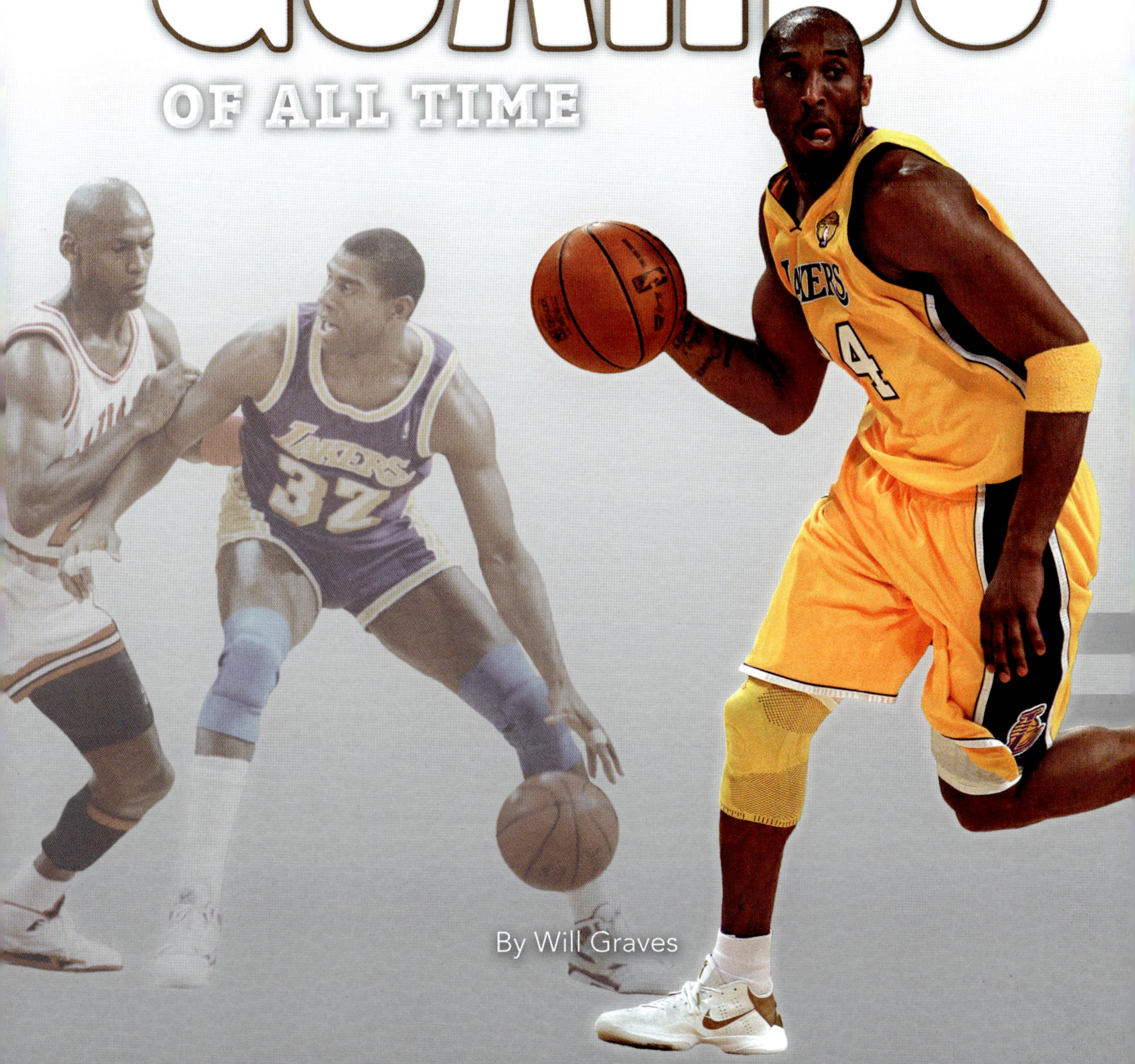

By Will Graves

www.abdopublishing.com

Published by Abdo Publishing, a division of ABDO, PO Box 398166, Minneapolis, Minnesota 55439.

Printed in the United States of America, North Mankato, Minnesota
032014
092014

THIS BOOK CONTAINS RECYCLED MATERIALS

Cover Photos: John Swart/AP Images (left); Jae C. Hong/AP Images (right)
Interior Photos: John Swart/AP Images, 1 (left); Jae C. Hong/AP Images, 1 (right); AP Images, 7, 9, 13, 17, 29; JWG/AP Images, 11; LA Times/AP Images, 15; Rusty Kennedy/AP Images, 19; Fred Jewell/AP Images, 21, 31; Reed Saxon/AP Images, 23, 25; Craig Fuji/AP Images, 27; Steve Wilson/AP Images, 33; Michael Conroy/AP Images, 35; Mark Duncan/AP Images, 37; Steve C. Wilson/AP Images, 39; Ron Schwane/AP Images, 41; Wilfredo Lee/AP Images, 43; John Fraschauer/AP Images, 45; Charles Krupa/AP Images, 47; Eric Gay/AP Images, 49; Donna McWilliam/AP Images, 51; Chris Carlson/AP Images, 53; Mark Avery/AP Images, 55; Mark J. Terrill/AP Images, 57; Nam Y. Huh/AP Images, 59; Charles Rex Arbogast/AP Images, 61

Editor: Chrös McDougall
Series Designer: Christa Schneider

Library of Congress Control Number: 2014932922

Cataloging-in-Publication Data
Graves, Will.
The best NBA guards of all time / Will Graves.
p. cm. -- (NBA's best ever)
ISBN 978-1-62403-412-1
1. National Basketball Association--Juvenile literature. 2. Guards (Basketball)--Juvenile literature. I. Title.
796.323--dc23

2014932922

TABLE OF CONTENTS

INTRODUCTION

For decades, basketball was a big man's game. Times sure have changed.

Most National Basketball Association (NBA) teams today are built around their guards. Shooting guards score a lot of points. Some of them like to slash to the basket. Others excel with picture-perfect jump shots. Point guards run a team's offense. They dribble the ball up the court. Then they find open teammates with laser-beam passes. Point guards thrive by making their teammates better. Being a great scorer is an added benefit. Many great guards are skilled at dribbling, passing, and shooting. The greatest guards often have one more skill: shutdown defense.

Here are some of the best guards in NBA history.

BOB COUSY

Bob Cousy's path to basketball greatness began with a bad break. While growing up in New York City, Cousy fell out of a tree. The fall broke his right arm. Cousy could not use his right arm while it healed. So he learned how to dribble and shoot a basketball with his left arm. The NBA was not prepared for what came next.

Cousy joined the Boston Celtics in 1950. He already was doing things that had never been done in games. He dribbled behind his back. He threw passes behind his head. He dribbled into the lane and threw up wild shots with either hand. And usually the shots went in.

It was just what the new league needed. The NBA had formed just four years earlier. And the Celtics had been one of the worst teams in it.

Boston Celtics guard Bob Cousy brings the ball past a New York Knickerbockers defender during a 1963 game.

BOSTON
14

Cousy helped turn around the Celtics' luck. They won six NBA titles in Cousy's 13 seasons.

One of Cousy's teammates called him a master on offense. Cousy could dribble his way out of trouble. He also was the league's best passer. His 6,955 careers assists were a record when he retired in 1970.

Cousy did more than just make fancy moves, though. He helped draw interest to the Celtics and the NBA. People wanted to see what new shot or pass Cousy would come up with next.

Above all else, Cousy was a winner. In 1963, the Celtics played the rival Los Angeles Lakers in the NBA Finals. Cousy had been injured in the fourth quarter of Game 6. His Celtics were trailing. Then Cousy ran back onto the floor and worked his magic. Minutes later, Boston and Cousy were once again champions.

8

The number of consecutive seasons, from 1952–53 to 1959–60, in which Bob Cousy led the NBA in assists. That was a record until John Stockton broke it in 1995–96.

The Celtics' Bob Cousy scores against the New York Knickerbockers in 1961.

BOB COUSY

Hometown: New York, New York

College: College of the Holy Cross

Height, Weight: 6 feet 1, 175 pounds

Birth Date: August 9, 1928

Teams: Boston Celtics (1950–63)
Cincinnati Royals (1969–70)

All-Star Games: 13 (1951–63)

Most Valuable Player (MVP) Award: 1956–57

First-Team All-NBA: 1951–52, 1952–53, 1953–54, 1954–55, 1955–56, 1956–57, 1957–58, 1958–59, 1959–60, 1960–61

OSCAR ROBERTSON

Guards were not supposed to look like Oscar Robertson. He was 6 feet 5 inches. Most coaches at the time would have stuck him at forward. The "Big O" was not like most forwards, though. He could shoot. He could dribble. And man, could he pass.

The triple-double is a rare feat in the NBA. It occurs when a player reaches double digits (10 or more) in three statistical categories in one game. Robertson took that to another level during the 1961–62 season. He averaged a triple-double each game. He put up 30.8 points, 12.5 rebounds, and 11.4 assists per game on the season. No other player in NBA history has come close to matching that feat through 2013.

Oscar Robertson of the Cincinnati Royals goes for a layup during a 1965 game against the Boston Celtics.

22
BOSTON
CELTICS
1964
EASTERN DIV
CHAMPIONS
CELTICS
15
CELTICS
6

Robertson was a nightmare to defend. He had too many skills. He would use his strength to bull his way to the basket against smaller guards. Or he would use his speed to leave bigger defenders flat-footed.

The only area in which Robertson did not excel was winning championships. He spent his first 10 seasons with the Cincinnati Royals. It was not until he was traded to the Milwaukee Bucks that he won his only title. Robertson joined the Bucks in 1970–71. There, he and center Lew Alcindor were a force together. Alcindor later changed his name to Kareem Abdul-Jabbar. The Bucks won 66 games that season. Robertson averaged 19.4 points and 8.2 assists. The Bucks swept the Baltimore Bullets in four games to win the NBA title.

9.5

Oscar Robertson's average assists per game for his career. Through 2013, that was the fourth-highest average in NBA history.

Robertson won just one title in his career. But his game paved the way for future oversized guards, including Earvin "Magic" Johnson.

The Royals' Oscar Robertson puts up a shot against the Chicago Bulls during a 1970 game.

OSCAR ROBERTSON

Hometown: Indianapolis, Indiana

College: University of Cincinnati

Height, Weight: 6 feet 5, 205 pounds

Birth Date: November 24, 1938

Teams: Cincinnati Royals (1960–70)
Milwaukee Bucks (1970–74)

All-Star Games: 12 (1961–72)

MVP Award: 1963–64

First-Team All-NBA: 1960–61, 1961–62, 1962–63, 1963–64, 1964–65, 1965–66, 1966–67, 1967–68, 1968–69

JERRY WEST

Three seconds remained in Game 3 of the 1970 NBA Finals. The Los Angeles Lakers trailed the New York Knicks by two points. That is when Lakers guard Jerry West took the inbounds pass. He dribbled a couple times. Then he pulled up from 60 feet (18.3 m) and flung the ball toward the basket. *Swish.*

The NBA did not have three-pointers until 1979. So West's miracle shot sent the game to overtime. The Lakers ended up losing the game and the series. But West's shot remains one of the most famous in NBA history.

West grew up in the small town of Chelyan, West Virginia. He spent countless hours as a child dribbling and shooting at a hoop in a neighbor's dirt driveway. He even played if it was raining or snowing.

Los Angeles Lakers guard Jerry West dribbles the ball down court against the Philadelphia 76ers in 1971.

LAKERS

West became a star guard at West Virginia University. He was named to the All-America team twice during college. The Lakers then picked him second overall in the 1960 NBA Draft.

West missed the 1971 playoffs due to injury. But the Lakers made the playoffs in each of West's 14 seasons. Nine times they made it all the way to the NBA Finals. However, West won just one NBA championship—in 1972. The Lakers had three Hall of Fame players on their team during that playoff run, including West. The team won a then-record 69 games. That included a 33-game winning streak that still stood in 2013.

27.0

Jerry West's career scoring average. It was the fifth highest in NBA history through 2013.

West shined even in defeat. The Lakers lost to the Boston Celtics in seven games in the 1969 NBA Finals. Yet West was named the Finals MVP.

The Lakers' Jerry West tries to dribble around a Houston Rockets defender during a 1971 game.

JERRY WEST

Hometown: Chelyan, West Virginia

College: West Virginia University

Height, Weight: 6 feet 2, 175 pounds

Birth Date: May 28, 1938

Team: Los Angeles Lakers (1960–74)

All-Star Games: 14 (1961–74)

First-Team All-NBA: 1961–62, 1962–63, 1963–64, 1964–65, 1965–66, 1966–67, 1969–70, 1970–71, 1971–72, 1972–73

All-Defensive Team: 1969–70, 1970–71, 1971–72, 1972–73

WALT "CLYDE" FRAZIER

A New York Knicks trainer gave Walt Frazier the nickname "Clyde." The nickname referred to famous bank robber Clyde Barrow. Barrow stole money from banks. And Frazier stole basketballs from opponents. Frazier was a great offensive player during his 13-year NBA career. But it was his defense that turned the Knicks into champions.

Former Knicks teammate Bill Bradley called Frazier an artist. That was not just because of the stylish clothes Frazier wore when he was not on the court. It was also because of the way he could glide through the lane on his way to a layup. But Frazier's biggest talent came at the other end of the floor. He would use his huge hands to swat, tip, or just flat out take the ball from an opponent.

New York Knicks guard Walt "Clyde" Frazier puts up a jump shot against the Philadelphia 76ers in 1976.

NEW YORK
10
COLLINS
20

Frazier could drive opponents crazy. He was blessed with quick hands and an aggressive attitude. Bradley said Frazier could "steal [the ball] any time he wants to." It sure seemed like it. He was the leader of a team that redefined defense on its way to two NBA titles.

Frazier and the Knicks won NBA titles in 1970 and 1973. Frazier was at his best in Game 7 of the 1970 Finals. He scored 36 points and dished out 19 assists. But it was his five steals that ultimately did in the Los Angeles Lakers. At one point, Frazier swiped the ball from Lakers star guard Jerry West and raced in for a layup. The play shook West, and the Lakers fell apart.

30

The number of points Walt "Clyde" Frazier scored during the 1975 NBA All-Star Game. He was named the game's MVP.

The Knicks' Walt "Clyde" Frazier dribbles around a Chicago Bulls defender during a 1972 game.

WALT "CLYDE" FRAZIER

Hometown: Atlanta, Georgia

College: Southern Illinois University

Height, Weight: 6 feet 4, 200 pounds

Birth Date: March 29, 1945

Teams: New York Knicks (1967–77)
Cleveland Cavaliers (1977–79)

All-Star Games: 7 (1970–76)

First-Team All-NBA: 1969–70, 1971–72, 1973–74, 1974–75

All-Defensive Team: 1968–69, 1969–70, 1970–71, 1971–72, 1972–73, 1973–74, 1974–75

EARVIN "MAGIC" JOHNSON

The Los Angeles Lakers needed a basket. They were down by a point in Game 4 of the 1987 NBA Finals. That is when Earvin "Magic" Johnson stole the show.

The Lakers' 6-foot-8 point guard dribbled into the lane. He lofted a high, arcing hook shot with his right hand. It was the kind of shot he rarely took. But of course it went in. It was Magic.

Lakers fans were used to such magic during the 1980s. The team was known as "Showtime" for its flashy play. The player nicknamed Magic was the star. He dazzled fans with his fancy passes and electric smile. It did not hurt that he also led the team to five NBA titles.

Johnson and Boston Celtics forward Larry Bird helped revive the NBA. The league was struggling when the two players entered in 1979.

Los Angeles Lakers guard Earvin "Magic" Johnson goes up for a hook shot against the Los Angeles Clippers in 1990.

Not many fans watched the games on television. The NBA Finals were not even broadcast live. Instead, they were taped and shown late at night. But the rivalry between Johnson and Bird helped change that.

Johnson put on shows with his passing. He could throw the ball the length of the court to find an open teammate. He could squeeze the ball between a sea of bodies in the lane. Or he could fool defenders with a perfect no-look pass. So Johnson once said, "Ask not what your teammates can do for you. Ask what you can do for your teammates." That was a play on a famous quote by former President John F. Kennedy.

10,141

The total number of assists Earvin "Magic" Johnson had during his career. It ranked fifth all-time through 2013.

Johnson became one of the most famous athletes on the planet. However, his career was cut short. He retired in 1991 after contracting the HIV virus. He returned briefly in 1996 before retiring for good.

Earvin "Magic" Johnson celebrates after his Lakers beat the Boston Celtics in the 1987 NBA Finals.

EARVIN "MAGIC" JOHNSON

Hometown: Lansing, Michigan

College: Michigan State University

Height, Weight: 6 feet 8, 215 pounds

Birth Date: August 14, 1959

Team: Los Angeles Lakers (1979–91, 1996)

All-Star Games: 12 (1980, 1982–92)*

MVP Awards: 1986–87, 1988–89, 1989–90

First-Team All-NBA: 1982–83, 1983–84, 1984–85, 1985–86, 1986–87, 1987–88, 1988–89, 1989–90, 1990–91

* Johnson came out of retirement to play in the 1992 All-Star Game

ISIAH THOMAS

Isiah Thomas did not look very intimidating. He stood just 6 feet 1 inch tall. He was not particularly muscular. Oh, and that smile. When Thomas smiled, he looked like an angel.

On the court, however, Thomas was a menace. He combined great speed and vision with an unending work ethic. The point guard was a skilled shooter and passer. Plus, he played shutdown defense. It is no wonder why Thomas's Detroit Pistons were one of the NBA's best teams in the late 1980s.

Thomas first put his Pistons on the map in 1988. The Pistons met the Los Angeles Lakers in the NBA Finals. Thomas badly sprained his ankle in the third quarter of Game 6. But he refused to sit out. Hobbling down the court, he found a way to finish with 43 points. His 25 third-quarter points were still an NBA Finals record in 2013.

Detroit Pistons point guard Isiah Thomas goes up for a basket against the Los Angeles Lakers in 1990.

LAKERS
14
11
4

The Lakers ended up winning a second consecutive NBA title that year. But Thomas and the Pistons made sure the Lakers did not win three in a row. Detroit beat the Lakers in the 1989 Finals. Then they beat the Portland Trail Blazers to win the 1990 title. Moreover, the Pistons beat the talented Michael Jordan and his Chicago Bulls in the playoffs all three of those seasons.

13.9

Isiah Thomas's assists per game in 1984–85. That was a career high and the most in the NBA that season.

The Pistons played with a hard-edged defense. That led to the nickname the "Bad Boys." And Thomas might have been the baddest of them all. He finished in the top five in the league in total steals three times during his career. Thomas proved that behind his boyish smile was a rugged defender.

The Pistons' Isiah Thomas gets ready to make a play against the New York Knicks during the 1992 playoffs.

ISIAH THOMAS

Hometown: Chicago, Illinois

College: Indiana University

Height, Weight: 6 feet 1, 180 pounds

Birth date: April 30, 1961

Team: Detroit Pistons (1981–94)

All-Star Games: 12 (1982–93)

First-Team All-NBA: 1983–84, 1984–85, 1985–86

CLYDE DREXLER

When Clyde Drexler jumped, he floated. He made the art of dunking look easy during his 15 seasons in the NBA. "Clyde the Glide" seemed to stay in the air while his opponents fell back to earth.

Drexler's dunking abilities were well known before he reached the NBA. He had played college basketball at the University of Houston. His teams there had been known as "Phi Slamma Jamma." They were famous for their players' abilities to slam the ball through the hoop.

Drexler carried that skill to the NBA. But dunking was hardly his only talent. During his career, he scored more than 20,000 points, grabbed more than 6,000 rebounds, and handed out more than 6,000 assists. Through 2013, he was one of only three players to rack up those numbers.

The Portland Trail Blazers' Clyde Drexler drives against the Chicago Bulls' Michael Jordan during the 1992 NBA Finals.

BLAZERS

However, Drexler's talent was sometimes overlooked. That can happen when you play in the era of Earvin "Magic" Johnson and Michael Jordan.

Drexler spent his first 11.5 NBA seasons in Portland. He helped the Trail Blazers become one of the NBA's best teams. Drexler led the Blazers to the NBA Finals in 1990 and again in 1992. The Blazers lost both times. But Drexler played courageously in defeat. He averaged 26.3 points during the 1992 playoffs. However, he could not find a way to beat Jordan and the Chicago Bulls.

27.2

Clyde Drexler's scoring average during the 1988–89 season, a career-high.

Things changed in 1994–95. The Blazers traded Drexler to the Houston Rockets. There he teamed with superstar center Hakeem Olajuwon. Drexler averaged 20.5 points in the playoffs that year. And the Rockets went on to sweep the Orlando Magic in the NBA Finals. Drexler finally was a champion.

Clyde Drexler, then with the Houston Rockets, goes up for a basket against the Utah Jazz during a 1995 game.

CLYDE DREXLER

Hometown: Houston, Texas

College: University of Houston

Height, Weight: 6 feet 7, 210 pounds

Birth Date: June 22, 1962

Teams: Portland Trail Blazers (1983–95)
Houston Rockets (1995–98)

All-Star Games: 10 (1986, 1988–94, 1996–97)

First-Team All-NBA: 1991–92

MICHAEL JORDAN

Michael Jordan was not always the best basketball player on his team. As a high school sophomore, Jordan did not even make the varsity team. But he made sure that never again happened.

Jordan developed into a star at Laney High in North Carolina. Then he won a national championship at the University of North Carolina. And he was just getting started. Jordan truly came into his own after joining the Chicago Bulls in 1984.

One of Jordan's first great moments in the NBA came during the 1988 Slam Dunk Contest. He soared from the free-throw line to win the title. He soon moved on to winning bigger titles. In 1992, Jordan helped Team USA win an Olympic gold medal. And between 1991 and 1998, he led the Bulls to six NBA titles. He was the NBA Finals MVP all six times.

Chicago Bulls guard Michael Jordan goes up for a dunk against the Indiana Pacers during a 1996 game.

NBA
BU
9
45

Jordan might have won more championships. However, he retired for a season and a half in the prime of his basketball career to pursue a baseball career. It was no surprise he came back to basketball. Jordan could do it all. He was one of the best scorers in NBA history. Yet he was just as good on defense. Jordan was named to the NBA All-Defensive first team nine times. He also won a pair of Slam Dunk Contest titles. But perhaps most importantly, he always seemed to rise to the moment.

"There's Michael Jordan," Earvin "Magic" Johnson once said. "And then there is the rest of us."

Jordan's stardom spread beyond the basketball court. He was one of the most popular athletes in the world and a commercial icon. Since retiring, Jordan has become the owner and chairman of the NBA's Charlotte franchise.

10

The number of NBA scoring titles Michael Jordan won. That was still an NBA record through 2013.

The Bulls' Michael Jordan drives to the hoop against the Cleveland Cavaliers during the 1989 playoffs.

MICHAEL JORDAN

Hometown: Wilmington, North Carolina

College: University of North Carolina

Height, Weight: 6 feet 6, 195 pounds

Birth Date: February 17, 1963

Teams: Chicago Bulls (1984–93, 1995–98)
Washington Wizards (2001–03)

All-Star Games: 14 (1985–93, 1996–98, 2002–03)

MVP Awards: 1987–88, 1990–91, 1991–92, 1995–96, 1997–98

First-Team All-NBA: 1986–87, 1987–88, 1988–89, 1989–90, 1990–91, 1991–92, 1992–93, 1995–96, 1996–97, 1997–98

All-Defensive Team: 1987–88, 1988–89, 1989–90, 1990–91, 1991–92, 1992–93, 1995–96, 1996–97, 1997–98

JOHN STOCKTON

There was nothing fancy about the way John Stockton played basketball. He did not make many behind-the-back passes. And he rarely took highlight-reel shots. That just was not Stockton's way. Instead, he made a career out of simply making the right play over and over again.

The Utah Jazz point guard spent 19 seasons as one of the steadiest players in the NBA. If a teammate got open, Stockton would get him the ball. Sometimes it was a bounce pass. Other times it was a chest pass. And other times still it was a baseball pass. It did not matter. Stockton just made sure that teammate got the ball. That is how he racked up 15,806 career assists. Through 2013, no player was within 3,000 of that total.

No teammate benefited more from Stockton's passing than power forward Karl Malone.

Utah Jazz point guard John Stockton heads down the court after a steal against the Dallas Mavericks in 1996.

Malone and Stockton worked very well together. It could be said that they formed the NBA's version of peanut butter and jelly during their 18 years together.

"There absolutely, positively will never ever be another John Stockton, ever," Malone said.

3,265

The number of steals John Stockton had in his career. That was an NBA record through 2013. However, steals were not recorded until 1973–74.

Stockton could do more than just pass. He also was sneaky on defense. He had a way of slipping his hands into passing lanes. Or he would pick an opponent's pocket to get the ball. Stockton also had a soft shooting touch. That showed in Game 6 of the 1997 Western Conference finals. He drilled a three-point shot at the buzzer. The basket sent the Jazz to the NBA Finals.

Stockton never won a championship. The Jazz lost to the Chicago Bulls in the 1997 and 1998 Finals. But that hardly tarnished the legacy of one of the NBA's all-time best passers.

The Jazz's John Stockton drives around a Cleveland Cavaliers defender during a 2003 game.

JOHN STOCKTON

Hometown: Spokane, Washington

College: Gonzaga University

Height, Weight: 6 feet 1, 170 pounds

Birth Date: March 26, 1962

Team: Utah Jazz (1984–2003)

All-Star Games: 10 (1989–97, 2000)

First-Team All-NBA: 1993–94, 1994–95

GARY

PAYTON

The only thing Gary Payton loved more than playing basketball was talking while he did it. He gave opponents an earful night in and night out during 17 very loud years in the NBA.

It helped that Payton's skills could back up his chatter. Payton did not just put up a hand to guard someone. He would smother an opponent. It was almost as if he was daring the player to try to beat him to the basket. That defensive effort earned Payton the nickname "The Glove."

Payton could score, too. He averaged more than 20 points per game in seven different seasons. But that is not what made him a star.

Seattle SuperSonics point guard Gary Payton goes up for a shot against the Miami Heat in 2002.

20
SONICS

Payton's quick hands and even quicker feet made him one of the best defenders in league history. He was named to the NBA All-Defensive first team every year between 1994 and 2002. And through 2013, he ranked fourth in league history with 2,445 steals.

2.9

Gary Payton's steals per game in 1995–96. That was a career best and the most in the NBA that season.

Payton began his NBA career with the Seattle SuperSonics. The team became a powerhouse behind him and high-flying forward Shawn Kemp. Seattle even reached the NBA Finals in 1996. However, the Sonics went on to lose to the Chicago Bulls.

Payton made it back to the Finals in 2004. This time he was with the Los Angeles Lakers. Again, however, Payton fell short of a title. He finally earned his first championship ring in 2006 while playing for the Miami Heat. In 2013, Payton was elected to the Basketball Hall of Fame.

The Sonics' Gary Payton runs the offense during a 2002 game against the Denver Nuggets.

GARY PAYTON

Hometown: Oakland, California

College: Oregon State University

Height, Weight: 6 feet 4, 180 pounds

Birth Date: July 23, 1968

Teams: Seattle SuperSonics (1990–2003)
Milwaukee Bucks (2003)
Los Angeles Lakers (2003–04)
Boston Celtics (2004–05)
Miami Heat (2005–07)

All-Star Games: 9 (1994–98, 2000–03)

First-Team All-NBA: 1997–98, 1999–2000

All-Defensive Team: 1993–94, 1994–95, 1995–96, 1996–97, 1997–98, 1998–99, 1999–00, 2000–01, 2001–02

JASON KIDD

The ball fell into Jason Kidd's hands. Kidd's New Jersey Nets teammates knew what to do. Forward Richard Jefferson took off running. Eventually, he looked back. Kidd was getting ready to pass the ball Jefferson's way.

There was a problem, though. Two defenders stood between Kidd and Jefferson. But to Kidd, that was no big deal. He threw a spinning, 40-foot (12.2-m) bounce pass. The ball hit the floor. It spun around the defenders. Finally, it landed right in Jefferson's hands. The result was an easy layup.

New Jersey Nets point guard Jason Kidd dribbles around a Boston Celtics defender during a 2006 game.

NEWJERSEY
5
30
vin' it

Kidd enjoyed passing to his teammates. In fact, his coaches sometimes had to ask him to shoot the ball every once in awhile. Kidd averaged just 12.6 points per game during his 19-year career. That is not a lot. But Kidd did not need to score to control the game. He was also a standout defender. Kidd led the NBA in total steals in 2001–02. He also led the league in assists per game five times.

12,091

The number of assists Jason Kidd had in his career. Only John Stockton had more through 2013.

Kidd could turn bad teams into great ones in an instant. The Nets had never made the NBA Finals. But then Kidd came along. He took the Nets to the Finals in 2002 and 2003. The Nets lost both times. However, Kidd did earn a championship ring with the Dallas Mavericks in 2011. The Mavericks beat the Miami Heat in the Finals. Kidd hit two three-point shots in Game 6 as Dallas won the title. As it turned out, Kidd could score when he wanted to.

Jason Kidd of the Dallas Mavericks drives around an Oklahoma City Thunder defender during the 2011 playoffs.

JASON KIDD

Hometown: Alameda, California

College: University of California

Height, Weight: 6 feet 4, 205 pounds

Birth Date: March 23, 1973

Teams: Dallas Mavericks (1994–96, 2008–12)
Phoenix Suns (1996–2001)
New Jersey Nets (2001–08)
New York Knicks (2012–13)

All-Star Games: 10 (1996, 1998, 2000–04, 2007–08, 2010)

First-Team All-NBA: 1998–99, 1999–2000, 2000–01, 2001–02, 2003–04

All-Defensive Team: 1998–99, 2000–01, 2001–02, 2005–06

STEVE NASH

Most kids in British Columbia, Canada, grow up wanting to play hockey or soccer. Steve Nash was no different. He could shoot a puck and kick a soccer ball. But his true talent was controlling a basketball.

At 6 feet 3 inches, Nash is not the tallest player on the basketball court. He also is not the fastest. But he was a solid dribbler and a great shooter. Plus, he always seems to find a way to make his teammates better. And that is the sign of a great point guard.

Nash debuted in the NBA in 1996 with the Phoenix Suns. He then played for the Dallas Mavericks for a few years. But he truly became a superstar when he returned to the Suns in 2004–05.

Phoenix Suns point guard Steve Nash passes under pressure against the Dallas Mavericks during the 2005 playoffs.

Nash was a perfect fit for the Suns' fast-paced offense. His favorite move was driving into the lane and then dribbling back out. Defenders usually followed him. That is when Nash would send a crisp pass to an open teammate, who would then take a shot. Those types of plays helped the Suns score a lot of points. Those plays also helped Nash win back-to-back MVP Awards in 2004–05 and 2005–06.

.904

Steve Nash's career free-throw percentage entering the 2013–14 season. It was the highest in NBA history.

Nash has a way of seeing plays two steps ahead. That is one of the reasons he led the NBA in assists five times between 2004–05 and 2010–11. His success has also helped make basketball more popular in Canada, where hockey is the national sport. In 2013, fellow Canadian Anthony Bennett was the first overall pick in the NBA Draft.

Every Canadian player, though, will have a long way to go to match Nash.

The Suns' Steve Nash goes up for a basket against the Dallas Mavericks during the 2006 playoffs.

STEVE NASH

Hometown: Victoria, British Columbia, Canada

College: Santa Clara University

Height, Weight: 6 feet 3, 195 pounds

Birth Date: February 7, 1974

Teams: Phoenix Suns (1996–98, 2004–12)
Dallas Mavericks (1998–2004)
Los Angeles Lakers (2012–)

All-Star Games: 8 (2002–03, 2005–08, 2010, 2012)

MVP Awards: 2004–05, 2005–06

First-Team All-NBA: 2004–05, 2005–06, 2006–07

KOBE BRYANT

It was January 22, 2006. The Los Angeles Lakers trailed the Toronto Raptors by 18 points in the third quarter. That is when Lakers guard Kobe Bryant got angry. And when he got angry, he got hot. By the final buzzer, the Lakers had won 122–104. Bryant scored 81 of those points. Only once had a player scored more points in a single NBA game.

"Not even in my dreams," Bryant said after the game. "That was something that just happened. It's tough to explain. It's just one of those things."

It often is just "one of those things" when it comes to Bryant. He entered the NBA straight out of high school in 1996. Bryant promised he could be the NBA's best player since Michael Jordan. In some ways, Bryant might have become even better.

Los Angeles Lakers guard Kobe Bryant goes up for a basket against the San Antonio Spurs during the 2008 playoffs.

20

It seems the bigger the game, the better Bryant plays. He led the Lakers to five NBA titles between 2000 and 2010. That is one fewer than the six Jordan won with the Chicago Bulls. Like Jordan, Bryant is not just a scorer. He is one of the best defenders of his time. He uses his long arms to frustrate opponents and get them off their game.

25.5

Kobe Bryant's career scoring average going into the 2013–14 season. That was the tenth best in league history.

Doing the same to Bryant is often impossible. He entered the 2013–14 season with 31,617 points. That was fourth on the NBA's all-time scoring list. And he can score his points in all kinds of ways. Bryant can dunk. He can pull up for a jump shot. He can hit three-pointers. And he can simply twist his way through the lane for a layup. Regardless, Bryant always seems to find the bucket.

The Lakers' Kobe Bryant dunks against the Utah Jazz during a 2013 game.

KOBE BRYANT

Hometown: Philadelphia, Pennsylvania

High School: Lower Merion

Height, Weight: 6 feet 6, 200 pounds

Birth Date: August 23, 1978

Team: Los Angeles Lakers (1996–)

All-Star Games: 16 (1998, 2000–14)

MVP Award: 2007–08

First-Team All-NBA: 2001–02, 2002–03, 2003–04, 2005–06, 2006–07, 2007–08, 2008–09, 2009–10, 2010–11, 2011–12, 2012–13

All-Defensive Team: 1999–2000, 2002–03, 2003–04, 2005–06, 2006–07, 2007–08, 2008–09, 2009–10, 2010–11

DWYANE WADE

Dwyane Wade was the forgotten man in the 2003 NBA Draft. LeBron James went first overall. Carmelo Anthony went third. Chris Bosh followed. It was not until the fifth pick that Wade heard his name called. He was going to Miami to play for the Heat.

All four players became stars in the NBA. But Wade was the first to become a champion. The Heat traded for superstar center Shaquille O'Neal before the 2004–05 season. And the very next year, Wade and O'Neal led the Heat to the first NBA title in team history. Wade averaged 34.7 points, 7.8 rebounds, 3.8 assists, and 2.7 steals in the Finals. It was one of the best all-around performances in Finals history.

Miami Heat guard Dwyane Wade drives to the hoop during a 2011 playoff game against the Chicago Bulls.

5
MIAMI
3

Wade is not a great shooter. Instead, he scores by crashing his way to the basket. He can beat just about any defender with his quickness. Plus, he can leap over bigger players to finish with a dunk. Wade also knows how to be a great teammate. That is a big reason why James and Bosh signed with Miami in the summer of 2010.

97

The number of free throws Dwyane Wade attempted in the 2006 NBA Finals. That was an NBA record through 2013.

Together, "The Big Three" became a force. They reached the NBA Finals in 2011. Then they won back-to-back NBA titles in 2012 and 2013. James was the biggest superstar on those teams. But there was little doubt that Wade was in charge.

"When you count him out and you need him most, the competition is at its fiercest moment, he's going to be there for you," Miami coach Erik Spoelstra said.

The Heat's Dwyane Wade dunks against the Chicago Bulls during the 2011 playoffs.

DWYANE WADE

Hometown: Chicago, Illinois
College: Marquette University
Height, Weight: 6 feet 4, 212 pounds
Birth Date: January 17, 1982
Team: Miami Heat (2003–)
All-Star Games: 10 (2005–14)
First-Team All-NBA: 2008–09, 2009–10

HONORABLE MENTIONS

Nate Archibald – Nicknamed "Tiny," Archibald was one of the NBA's first great scoring point guards. Through 2013, Archibald was the only player to lead the NBA in points and assists in the same season, which he did in 1972–73.

George Gervin – Called the "Iceman" because he was so smooth, the 6-foot-7 Gervin led the NBA in scoring four times and missed the All-Star Game just twice in a 14-year career, most of which was played with the San Antonio Spurs.

Allen Iverson – "AI" was known for a devastating crossover dribble. Despite being just 6 feet tall, Iverson averaged 26.7 points during his career and won the MVP Award while leading the Philadelphia 76ers to the NBA Finals in 2001.

Sam Jones – Jones won 10 NBA championships while playing for the Boston Celtics from 1957 to 1969. The five-time All-Star averaged 17.7 points across 12 seasons.

Pete Maravich – "Pistol Pete" was one of the NBA's all-time great showmen. He averaged a record 44 points per game in college at Louisiana State University and was a five-time All-Star during the 1970s with the Atlanta Hawks and the New Orleans Jazz.

Reggie Miller – One of the best shooters in NBA history, Miller made 2,560 three-pointers during his career—the second-highest total ever through 2013. He was a five-time All-Star during his 18 seasons with the Indiana Pacers from 1987 to 2005.

Chris Paul – A fantastic passer and outstanding ball handler, Paul helped turn the lowly Los Angeles Clippers into championship contenders when he was traded to the team in 2011.

Lenny Wilkens – Truly a coach on the floor, Wilkens was a nine-time All-Star for four teams between 1960 and 1975. He went on to win 1,332 games during a 32-year coaching career. That was a record when he retired.

GLOSSARY

assist
A pass that leads directly to a basket.

defense
The act of trying to stop your opponent from scoring a basket.

draft
A system used by leagues to spread incoming talent throughout the teams.

rebound
A recovery of a missed shot.

rookie
A first-year player in the NBA.

steal
A statistic awarded to a player who takes the ball away from an opponent or intercepts a pass intended for an opponent.

veteran
A player with a lot of experience.

FOR MORE INFORMATION

Further Readings

Schaller, Bob, and Dave Harnish. *The Everything Kids' Basketball Book.* Avon, MA: Adams Media, 2009.

Silverman, Drew. *Basketball.* Minneapolis, MN: Abdo Publishing Co., 2012.

Silverman, Drew. *The NBA Finals.* Minneapolis, MN: Abdo Publishing Co., 2013.

Websites

To learn more about NBA's Best Ever, visit **booklinks.abdopublishing.com**. These links are routinely monitored and updated to provide the most current information available.

INDEX

ABOUT THE AUTHOR

Will Graves grew up in a family of basketball players and wanted to be like John Stockton. Instead, he ended up writing about players instead of playing alongside them. He has covered sports since 1996 and joined The Associated Press in 2005. He spent six years covering basketball in hoops-mad Kentucky and now works in Pittsburgh, Pennsylvania, where he finds time to play pickup games every once in awhile.